FAITH

FAITH

Lynne McMahon

Wesleyan University Press
Middletown, Connecticut

"Missouri Box-Step" is for Lois and Dean McMahon.
"The Paris Women's Peace March" is for Carol Muske.
"In the Garden" is for Charles Wright.

Some of the poems in this book appeared previously in: *American Poetry Review, Antioch Review, The Atlantic Monthly, Black Warrior Review, Field, The Iowa Review, New England Review and Bread Loaf Quarterly, Open Places, Prairie Schooner, Quarterly West, Raccoon.*

All inquiries and permissions requests should be addressed to the Publisher, Wesleyan University Press, 110 Mt. Vernon Street, Middletown, Connecticut 06457.

Distributed by Harper & Row Publishers, Keystone Industrial Park, Scranton, Pennsylvania 18512.

LIBRARY OF CONGRESS
CATALOGING-IN-PUBLICATION DATA

McMahon, Lynne.
   Faith.
√ (Wesleyan new poets)
   I. Title. II. Series.
PS3563.C3856F3   1988   811'.54   86-32440
ISBN 0-8195-2133-7 (alk. paper)
ISBN 0-8195-1135-8 (pbk. : alk. paper)

Manufactured in the United States of America

FIRST EDITION

Wesleyan New Poets

for Rod

Contents

I

Calm

The wisteria and honeysuckle, beaten
for hours by the rain and wind,
slowly unmold from the trellis, slowly
take back their purple from the white wood

and begin again a synthesis of scent and pollen.
The frogs, too, are out, and the snakes
from under the porch begin their perilous
S descent to the bayou. We're the last to get up,

reluctant to leave our crouch in the middle
of the floor where we listened to the sea
that was one town over break over us. We could
taste the metal in the air, could almost touch

the cave dweller from our shrouded past
whose genetic legacy made us immortal.
We had been reading when the furies
first let go in immense noise;

and in the sudden quiet, which was either
the end of the storm or its eye, everything
seemed vast and distant, like the space around
Prince Andrei, so removed at the novel's end,

so far from the ones he loved, who loved him,
that their touching, hurrying cries were less
than the breath of wind muttering
high up in the eaves of his childhood house—

a memory of breath that sounded faintly
in the white tunnel of concentration
carrying him faster and faster
toward a soundless buoy of light.

Hawaiian Shirt

Like a tourist's joke, I think, some
             gift brought back for the home-
bound or suit-and-tie wearers,
except he's wearing it, smiling into the non-
             exotic airport lounge,
and as he approaches I can tell

it's hand-painted, the design
             continuous over seams
and breast pocket, and isn't a joke.
I nearly speak—as if to ask him—but
             something in our embrace,
or the figures and vibrancy

of the colors, works its way
             around me, vertiginous,
subverting the text like cathedral
windows: there are coconuts here, dropping
             forever into the basket
of the bare-legged girl

who has planted her machete
             in the red earth.
She is laughing up at the boy
in the tree, leaf-sliced into brown
             and green and yellow
bars, his shirt a purple flag

signaling the canoe that curves
             into sight
from the back's horizon—
they are waiting for sunset, the end
             of the day's labor,
when they can glide into

the spectacular surf, gone
red and gold,
together. The background cloth
feels like muslin, so soft I press my face
into it,
to hear it breathe,

to hear his heart beneath it,
and think
how lucky he is to walk around
in a story so beautiful, and so often
repeated, it must
once have been true.

Resort

Worse than Niagara Falls, this endless
susurration of surf over crowds
of retirees and honeymooners,
steel guitar piped into the elevator,
and palm fronds in the gin-and-tonics . . .

Our hotel room's one step from the ice
machine, a tiny avalanche every twenty-
five minutes and the odd end-
of-the-world crash as the scoop descends,
but the window opens on a true earth-fall

of bougainvillaea, so dense we see
the sky in chinks, blue
flecks of light behind the red, wind-
stirred bells, and that's enough
to put us in the mind of the place:

the lemon carpet and parrot shower
curtain are themselves emblems of
the rain forest this room was
millennia ago. The crust traveling
in green procession from the spigot

to the bung of the basin
began its journey in the high fog-falls
of Eden, and the ancient, odorless
microbes clustering beneath the safety
label on our water jar clustered here

when jaguars did. What civilization
is amassing itself in the pink sandstone
blocks thrown out against the sea?
What choiring of island birds? It's all
here for future excavation,

though what was once tar, and before
that excoriated wood or coal, has become
Duranyl, and what was once a mundane leaf
spine fossilized into museum quartz is now
a child's handprint on the cement drive.

Ninth Month

The machine for lowering the body
into bed, the mechanical armchair that propels
      the sitter into a half-crouch
and then a stand, the chair

    affixed to the bannister
that rides to the second floor of the grand house
      in the old movie;
La-Z-Boy, Stand Again, Walkabout—

    the names alone could transport me
from the land of health to the infinitely
      more complicated land
of the half-capacitated.

    It must have been the exhaustion
of childhood—too many wagon races or hard
      miles on the bike—
that made this animate furniture

    the sum of what could be aspired to.
And I saved toward it: the sleep lost
      to slumber parties and camp,
deoxygenated blood

    and flagging lungs after asthma
attacks, all-night novels, all-night bashes,
      nights lost
to Dexedrine, to anxiety, to love—

    the account all the while
accruing in the gray fog bank of exhaustion
      which I am at last
closing out. Thirty years of tiredness

are descending to anchor
my feet, lost somewhere beneath the curve
of this lodged, undersea,
weighted balloon. I'm ready. I'm settling

forever into the depths of this chair
to ponder the great gift of my fatigue until
the electricity resumes
or help arrives to lift me up.

The New Days

for my son

Nothing warned me of the new days,
How the stars would open their mouths
And the nights cry
And the flowers tremble on their feathery necks
Until I came with my gift.

                Only five months and already
It's hard to place myself in that slap of the sea
And the burnt breath of Los Angeles folding
Around its hills. It's there, but only
         as memory, locked away like his bear
In the lucite cage,
The starfish sleeping on blue foam beside him,

Something to be returned to after the night's journey—
        this photograph of Carol and Mark
    and the two of us fixed and smiling
           before the new days.

       *   *   *   *   *

Peril
    is the key to this house.
That beautiful word slips like a pearl
To the floor of the bathtub,
Rolls off under the crib where the arm bends backward,

It sews itself to the eye of the lion.

    Swallow me, it sings,
Its voice as sweet as honey-hunting Pooh's
           luring the face to press itself
    unliftably from the earth—

Poor nightmare parents! Caught between
Breath and breath,
Taking on a cyanotic luster in the dark hollow . . .

   So I read novels.
"Little Mother," I call myself,
Hugging my breasts.
     Here is my Russian kerchief
  and the heavy cans of goat's milk sloshing from the barn.

This is the good life,
Levin's farm in a good year,
    uncomplicated,
  and hundreds of pages before Anna's little boy
      is abandoned.
The peasant stirs her jam in the great kitchen,
Her child dimples and waves his fat hands
   to the iron pot.
     Morning
  is early here, rising in the haycocks,
—a breakfast of bread soaked in dippered well water—

But under the morning, the pearly track.
Beneath the pure sky, the whisper.

   * * * * *

"I feel it is an omen," the woman says.
But everything is.
The sun hurts so much the phlox collapses
   and the birds hop distractedly
   on the burning bath.

Look, Benjamin,
                    see how the cardinal is losing his looks,
                    see how the jay ignites.

If I were shade I would revive them. If I were water
                    they could drink.
          The glass protects us for now, kissed
                    to his moist forehead and palm,
But there are three floors—
                            the seeds drop,
                            the walnuts drop—

My arms reach out and down through midges and milkweed,
                    scooping ruin from the brick porch,
And the voice of the bad queen starts up in the cicadas.

              *   *   *   *   *

Some beds grow more familiar
The less we sleep in them. Carved pine cones
              and grapes in the headboard of this one
      I touched in dreams years ago,
And the crib quilt with its wheels and flags.

He likes to be read to here, cadences falling
Like soft hammers
                    till he is pounded into sleep. Here,
          the mantra doesn't matter,
The chant does not begin Diphtheria, Pertussis, Typhoid—

The ghosts of other small bodies turn
                    as his turns, the same rootings,
          damp ovals on the flannel sheet.

What mother could bear to love her child
                knowing, in sixty years, what he would become?
But Yeats was wrong to ask. It's not a question.
                Michelangelo's Pietà is closer—
        the marble fact of her son's body,
        heavy with mortality,
And her face beyond dreaming.
                                Her one purpose—
        to protect, always to protect—
                                gone.
What promise of redemption could ever make that right
        again?
Juno spilled her milk across the heavens
And still the galaxies cry.

                *   *   *   *   *

All night the window has kept
                its black square intact—my lamp and chair
        doubled and given back in its frame,

"The Nursery at Midnight" inked in . . .

All the little ones I never had keep vigil with me—
Drawstrings tucked, sleeves folded back
                so the hands can move.
        They are ready for the lunge, the sudden breathless stop,
But for now they want their starlight, glasses of milk,
                story.
I think I shall tell them my favorite—it's called
Morning
                and it licks at the floorboards,

Sending its little by little to the edge of the rug,
              then the whole rug,
                      then the crib is ringing
        with light and Ben is singing it,
Chasing it across the bumper and bars and sheets—

How easy everything is in this version!
The bear rumbles in his glass house, then settles,
              content to be there,

The pelican bounces on his springy chain,

The sky is swept clean of everything
              but one wing slicing the air
                      on the way to another branch

Where Pooh has returned the honey
And Anna emerges intact from the shadow of the train.

        Flowers everywhere are licked into color
And it is morning, ordinary and amazing.

Asthma

Tremors, and yet my son
    Demands to play, to climb
Onto my knees, his Everest.
    The air begins thinning out

In white sockets around his eyes
    Which closes my throat too. *Rest now,*
I want to tell him, which only makes him angry
    And scared. I have gasped that way

In nightmares, muffled in feathers and wool,
    But my bones never took on
Such prominence. His shoulders work
    Their wingbones and his ribs

Open and close like palm fronds
    In some terrible fan. And still he rises,
Putting his hand against my face
    And finding my lap two logs

On which to roll, not falling,
    His small heart and my larger one
Jerking out their mismatched rhythms.
    But now it is my breath

Which begins the hard ascent,
    And I am the mountain after all,
Locked by the snow's embrace, the blue veins,
    And remote clouds which are not moving.

Faith

Although what shimmers
in this white corridor
is only a short
in the fluorescent
tubes, and what sounds
like a celestial chorus
only pneumatic doors
sucking the air, some-
thing about the light
and music of this place
is beautiful. We smile
because we're not here
for anything serious
and because everything
around our child amuses
instead of frightens
him: his gown, the
color of fluorocarbons
or bluish milk, billows
around him like a wave,
as if the gurney were
afloat and carrying
him toward sound,
or toward some high
vibration that will
become a sound spending
itself against the glut
at the bone wall. Only
the thinnest frayed
end brushes the tympanum
and bulge of water
which swells then
ebbs at the shore of
the brain, the strand

that connects him
to the one round
syllable that is
his name. It's what
I imagine prayer must
be—church the hollow
cavern, the sounding
room in the head
of God, and liturgy
a muffled sibilance until
intercession. Faith,
like the tiny metal
tubes, mere mica flecks
in the doctor's palm,
works its miracle
by engineering: the wedge
placed between mucosum
and drum opens a seam
in the rock that is
the skull, and the plaints
and singing are let in.

II

Toussaint

In France, it begins in the Atlantic,
shivering October phosphor gathering over the backs
of whales and cormorants, a bank of spirits moving
east in a phalanx held wide and flat as the shore.
And here, at the shore, they pause, lifting just above
the sand so the water can lie down and stand up,
lie down and stand up without mixing its element
with the nacreous other. At the signal star,
they move. Some to fishing villages and farms,
others to the acres of grapes curling to the base
of mountains—mine come narrowing finally
to this strip of Seine, the frosted cakes of buildings
stacked on either side, indifferent. But the tourist
barges pull against their wedded ropes and moan.

For they come riding, gliding on the oily current,
confiding to the air vaporous soliloquies
and holding out their tatters of fog in a gesture
so nearly human the worm in the heart retreats.
This must be the last guise of memory, pared
to a wraith and shaken out just once a year
to shrive itself among the littered walkways
and socket eyes of saints. They're the opaque mirrors
to no future, a past we only half imagine—all
souls, even the ones we are named for, disconnected
from the bodied dreamer. Poor dead. And poor us
who pocket their opalescent tears.

Patois

Père-Lachaise Cemetery, Paris

What led us here was more accident than prayer,
Though a wind that could have been a prayer kept paging

Through the missal left at the base of the Haitian
Seer's stone. We had been looking for Proust

And Colette in this quadrant of sepulchres
When a sound like sea-surge, a moan of surf,

Began. It was the wind, we thought, which
Having no trees to claw, or water or grasses

To record its passing, had devised a keening
Against the corner monuments.

There was the voice of the drowned in it, a spray
Of foreign voices abandoned in the air

Between the lowering sky and marble doves, a not-quite
French that rose and lowered in the sea-salt

Cadenced forever, forever. Then it was done. The knot
Of worshipers undid itself and stepped out

Of the circle of fire the plastic flowers made
And the singing stopped. We became more

Northern then, following the white clouds of our
Breath back to the Métro, away from the stones

And the dark vortex of that island song. When birds
Lift from the pediments it must be like that:

The earth's magnetic field tugging at the trace metal
In their skulls, drawing them through

The migratory arc from sea to land
Like a Carib priest summoning his voodoo back.

Our First Porno Movie

We were lucky enough to see a good one,
If good is the right word,
A beautiful iconography:
The colors of Vermeer damascened
Against a sky and lake and boulevard
So motionless it could have been a set piece—

Swann spying in on the music students,
At that oblong of thigh against the velvet banquette,
Or any bit of Victoriana viewed through the stereopticon.
No threat anywhere, no sign
That the universe of the usual was about to be
Branded and knotted with silk thongs,

Women turning slowly by the wrists
Or chained one to another at the long
Glass table topped with pears and plums
And of course the blushing peach—
It was roundness bitten into.
Our first recorded sin playing itself over and over

Centuries past the original thrill,
Past memory of motive,
Save perhaps in the vestigial ache
At the back of the tongue
Which says those long afternoons in Paradise
Were too long.

How else to explain the transparent robes
Of the woman in the owl's mask, gorgeous
At the prow of the rowboat,
Her feathers stirred slightly by the motion of oars
As they dipped and shimmered toward some French sacrifice,
Except to say that incongruity and desire,

The disjunction between body and soul,
Is at the heart of knowledge:
We know now what we are not—
Not owl or angel or plane of light
But object dropped
From the mind of God into dark movie houses

Where the rustle of cloth against cloth
Grows first to a growl, then a roar,
Then an enormous pulse of tearing air
Rushing to fill
Whatever space has been left open
Once the lid to heaven is snapped shut.

Notre-Dame

1.

Afloat in its stone boat, moored to either shore
by the openwork stockings of bridges,

it isn't what I imagined for her. Not
her phial of tears and the crystal firmament, not

even serenity, but something like power
drawn in and waiting, stone buttresses rayed out

in spiders and that northwest gargoyle
caressing a pediment knobbed like the knuckle

of a huge arthritic Lucifer left a slash of air
where the spire once stood.

2.

Even when I thought I listened, I heard only my
dressed-up versions. And Joyce scuffing in the dust

offstage: There is no God and Mary is His
Mother. Because stone carved as a monument to grief

can't tell the whole story. We ask for the bruised
flesh to walk out of the headlines and back

to his village—the lens of the sun transfiguring
the fissured earth, but rainfall come again.

This is one corner of the holy card, written
in the white space between the gilt and the flower.

3.
I have decided to list it once, then let it go:
this street, river, knife found under the radiator,

this misstep in the dark, stumble against the stone,
armies of microorganisms twisting their way

up the canal of the spine, fluid collecting
in the interstices, and stupid love fluting away.

Now we enter the quiet world where millions go on
and there are no black stars in the ledger.

This is the official version. This coat of warm honey
whose sleeves are weighted and sweet, too heavy to lift.

4.
It's my son who brings me to this vast transept
when the secular consolings fail. We require

a salve for the hurt place, and beyond that,
no hurt place. A future swept clean

in the power of incantation. Together we trace out
the letters, beginning to spell the spell. Love

assembles in clouds above the parapet, rainfall come
again, and bits of bread on the ledge when the storm clears.

God's architect commissioned stone trees for the birds
and slits in the tower where Benjamin lays his hand.

5.
When the crane swings into motion, I see the quay
recast by spring, giant toys in orange and blue

intriguing with history. First digs. Birth of the ancient.
Mossed stones crumbling. And Notre-Dame like

an immense surveyor whose chalk lines extend
past the slatted boards of the barricade to the base

of St. Genevieve, where every afternoon the same teenager
plays his air guitar. The first green of the chestnuts

blows open its canopy and I forget awhile, dawdling
along the concrete wall, forgetting to close my hands.

6.
The morning's last treasure, a chip of marble
nicked out by chance or vandals, its place

appropriated now by grime and river wind. For me,
it is all of Paris—this massive cathedral

jagged and weightless in my hand, and Vivaldi
leaking out through the iron hinges. A rehearsal

for joy, like the silver ozone we're flying into. Home
is the new century, pure and statueless—electrons

whirling in the cloud chamber. We edge our furtive selves
inside, refitting the stone drop in the angel's eye.

In the English Countryside

Charred, an oval of black grass
Where the plane went down,

Its delicate egg of orange light
Wobbling a moment before the spill

Onto the field—
A Halifax, the village kids

Speculate, or maybe a Lancaster.
And their mothers, overhearing,

Are jarred again by the wartime
Lexicon they've become, in time,

So fluent in. The syllables roll
Over the tongue, unbearably sweet,

Made just bearable by the determinedly
Flat pronouncement. For to acknowledge

The pleasure of *contrail*
Or *fuselage* is to undermine

The high seriousness of being boys
In England, in the countryside,

In 1944. Is to demote
The almost-ready-to-serve

To the ranks of children who are
Less than anything, vaulting

The last stile into the neighbor's
Field where the blackened

Grass, like a magic circle,
Holds the Lancaster and its sheared

Wing. This is the fairy tale,
The past. And over there, behind

The trees, the future is untying
His tally-strings.

From the white canopy, to keep
The fragile silk aloft.

The Paris Women's
Peace March

As if the fact of gender alone
        Could halt the spin
Of the earth and seize,

        As in myth,
The upswept banners fluttering
        In carnival procession

For the dead or soon
        To disappear
And unfurl them before the gods;

        As if there were gods
To petition, and the sky once
        More the floor

Of heaven where edict
        Writes itself
In the underlit cumulus;

        As if there were Mercy,
We take into our massed body
        The rhetoric

And buzzing microphones,
        Fatigue climbing
The spine to the outermost

        Shoulders
Where white placards tilt
        And sway like thousands

Of unpaired wings, as if
        Flight were simply
A matter of faith.

Futureworld

What happens in the transformation
of airplane to robot-man—gray
plastic nose cone to cone-like
helmet, wings folded out into sharp
shoulders—might be an acknowledgment
by the toy czars that there exists
some ancient law in the ancient realm
beneath the kitchen table, that little
boys can manipulate death-weapon
into escape-mobile, and thereby
hold off the last convulsions
of a rapidly fading, gray-edged planet.

It makes sense to see it like that,
as training ground in the superreal.
For after the stacking blocks and clay
presses, after the giant Crayolas
rolling in brilliant wrappers in
and out of the junk drawer, after
the long practice in motor skills,
what better skills? The ailerons/
knee joints lock into place,
and flight becomes stiff-gaited
advance, the steely underbelly
a flak jacket breastplate
harboring the secret dials and codes
wired to the brain of a three-year-old
who says You can look now, Mommie.
Because he's turned up the light.

III

In the Garden

1/ Earth

They are incontrovertible, the evidences
Of spring. How completely the robin clears
The lip of the feeder and ground beneath.
How intent the cat is, advancing on the mole
Over the invisible grubs that feed it
In the dark excavations. Pushing
The lawn mower over a yard gone spongy with
Tunnels, you think only fleetingly
Of the first salt sweating down your back
Like the mysteries of origin, while your gloves,
Braced against the shudder of the grips, curl
And hold fast, guiding you past the tall trees
Which are the demarcations of Paradise.

2/ I Know Two Birds

The swallow, but only in flight,
    And the male cardinal.
Oh, I'm right about the blue jay
    And pigeon, of course,
But in the aviary of timeless
    Splendor
They are the commoners,
    As I am,
Visitor,
    Dragging the ferrule of
My umbrella past
    Students with their sketchpads
Encamped here because the daylight
    Lasts past nine.

So I can't describe these
    Beyond the brown
Uniform
    Sometimes broken by
Yellow bars
    Or eye rings,
But the song, the song
    Goes on revolving
In the deepening bowl of the sky.
    It undresses the earth
For the bath, holds out
    The thick uncurtained moonlight
Laying down its wing
    To lay me down to sleep.

3/ Toward Eve

Up the cement steps and cracked
Sidewalk with its hairline of grass, up
The wood ramp to the porch which is
Beginning a slow sag and rotting
Just perceptibly in the crosshatch
Of latched sticks on the underside,
Off in the shadiest corner contracted
Against the light—this
Is where you kneel. This is the first
Morning after the sea's departure,
After the fish spines adding their nitrogen
To the loam, after the plankton.
In tiny knuckles of upturning life,
The ferns push up into their brains,
Pushing, straightening, finally one morning
(In the thousand hours of the first
Morning) no longer the green sea horses
Of infant plants. They are astride
The earth now, tall
In their first arrogance. The book
Doesn't say how soon they will bend
To the soil and the hidden nocturnal
Creatures beneath. On that, the book
Is silent, as the ferns are, as the woman
Is who stoops to direct their waters, tending
And blending in, as on the sixth day.

4/ Empire

And there were, in the garden,
Dutch iris, beautifully
        Ugly,
The purple underlip
    (Which the grower's guide
Calls a beard)
        Sun-drugged, dragged
Earthward
    So the corolla might rise
Like a wand, producing
        The fretwork
Of sun motes and water
    In a presto of light.
Imperious,
        Cared-for,
Sown in cold frames or protected
    Seedbeds and left
To sojourn beneath
        The indoor lights—
A nursling slip
    Gardening the skies.
Roses bloomed
        Above the jungle—
But that was years ago.
    Cluster carriers opened
Their calyx
        And petals fell,
Years ago.
    From heaven, the Western World
Is a purple/blue on the map.
        Such a proud flower
Fretting the sun
    To water, water to the grid
That was the earth.

Missouri Box-Step

The box-step is the only step I know so
   I'm teaching it to him. The corners
Are tricky, the entire move is tricky,
   All angle and swoop ruined
If you smear over the turn and slide
   Too soon.

My parents move in this body, mounting
   The air stairs to the top of my head
Then down again, trailing the bannister
   Of my spine, marking their perfect time.
Her shoes were always perfectly inside his,
   Her elbow a bend of cloud in his palm—

They were so beautiful I wanted to stay
   Forever in *Begin the Beguine*
And *String of Pearls*. Later, of course,
   The scene changed. The scrim
Became floodlit by my own entry
   Into the circle of arms and the brain's

New constellated furor—prom lights
   And the sweet inelegant press, mouths
Slightly open and whispering against my neck.
   But this was before my own arrival,
Before the years of falling
   Into the tumult of slow dancing

Where every gesture arrowed into desire's place,
   Until desire staggered like Kurosawa's hero
Into the fog of the completed act.
   This was not yet sex, but connection
Of a different order. Something wholly
   Contained, but given over as well

To the child who watched, to our child
　Who wants to curve himself around us
And become his parents dancing.
　For him, it is the rightness of the thing,
The singularity of the square world
　Which is familial

And secret in the spores of generation.
　For us, it is time regained; living-room
Ballrooms whose pool of lamplight and shadow-
　Nets catch us up in a swirl of memory
And anticipation for what the morning reveals
　And the night amplifies.

To Save Summer

It's July, too early
for yellow leaves drizzled
        over a green lawn

        but there they are, unrefuted
by the heat, already dead
        and, like any dead, out

        of season. Walnuts pock
the dirt like emblems dropped
        for squirrels

        who aren't prepared yet
to pack or deconstruct them and it's
        weird, as if the earth's

        axis shifted overnight,
one cycle accelerating into another,
        and time shortened itself.

        It's not a true explanation,
I know, but the best I can offer
        when he comes in

        demanding a castle and cliff,
something gigantic, and I point him
        toward the arbor—

        that waterfall of yellow
leaves and the unexpected seed-pod
        artillery

are immensity of a kind—
and he runs happily toward it,
feeling in his footsoles

the precipitate slide
of the earth toward autumn
which could be

the work of moles
the size of dragons tunneling
to the core of the globe,

bending the rod
that pierces it, and he's the lucky
one charged with flinging

himself on the ground
to hold it in place,
to save summer.

Unbuilding

Stepping around bales
of fencing wire and a clutter
of machine parts on my way
to class

I stopped to watch two men
on top of the building next to mine
tossing rectangles
of old or damaged asphalt

sheets off the roof and
into the bed
of a red pickup parked
four floors below on the grass.

I stopped
out of habit, to give
odds on a miss—one out of ten
seemed right—but these two

never missed. They had
a rhythm going. Their bandanas,
fastened over nose
and mouth, dipped

and swung up as their arms did,
the whole torso
curving then straightening
over their braced legs,

and one gold earring,
the taller man's, flashing out
as if it were itself charged
with movement

and music. There might have been
music—a Walkman, perhaps—but I
        couldn't hear it.
    There must certainly have been

carcinogens and bitumen scruff
        floating up from the tiles,
    but I couldn't see it.
From the ground, it was purely

        beautiful. Two men
    in silhouette against a noon-
blazed blue, lifting and releasing
        like blue work-

    shirted angels
clearing the sky of decades of
        dust, so the day's
    work might begin again.

Rippled Window

Drawn through panels of glass, elongated
Beak, then breast, then last foreshortened
Tail feather, the bird on the other
Side distorts to two then one
As the branch distorts—a fun house
Horizontal framed in 1905 when the house
Was built. Some fault in the silica
Compound, or the firing, left
The glaze imperfect, but close enough
To call transparent. And for eighty
Years clouds and tree limbs have swum
Through an illusion of chopped time—
Movement jerking forward and back
Like the pages of a flip-book
Whose characters animate at the hands'
Whim. It's my whim now. Mistress
Of this house and window whose
Casement opens on a bird-crossed
Sky and three white chairs below,
I direct the surface, pressing it
To yield a new angle or shine. It's
The carnival slyness I love—the solidity
Of Victorian thought giving way to a crazed
Window, perfecting that metaphor in what
Matthew Arnold called Sweetness
And Light. For it is sweet to make
The bird more than her parts, or all her
Parts in sequence. And when
She flies off beyond the frame into
A light not yet broken into prisms
By the glassmaker's stumble,

That might be sweeter still. But what
Moves beyond this air
Is unimaginable.
I want the real weirdness. Come back,
Bird. Come back, funny sunlight.

Autumnal

Kicking up the leaves some thoughtless
Or thoughtful neighbor left unraked
On the sidewalk and lip of driveway, I stopped
To look for some silvery thing I caught
The edge of, which disappeared as I bent down.
Some angle of light, I suppose, or fracted

Movement which rasped the cerebellum and sent
Red motes streaking across my retina
Blotted out everything but blood and swirling
Silvery fishes, sending me headlong in slow-
Motion to the ground. Whatever was gone wrong
In the cortex and nerve endings was made right

In the world: the child's ring I fished for was
Inches from my head. The half-hidden suddenly sharp
And up close, the pan over the street and yard
(Forty-five degrees, all I could manage) in soft
Focus, I swung away and back to the morse of glints
I knew I could decode if only the film speeded up. I

Wanted to hasten the conclusion, see myself gathering
Then kneeling, then standing up—my head steady
In its orbit of rings, a light almost a halo
Circling in the blown leaves around me. But what
I felt was the pavement pressing up through my
Pea coat and scarf, the cold recalling me to the ordinary

Where I was enjoined to release the ring, the film,
The astronomy of meanings whose secrets I was
Allowed to enter, for a moment, and immediately
Forget. I was too quick for the gift then, or the earth
Was too heavy. But now, when the seasons turn, I stand
Still, willing the seizure, and the fall.

The Lighthouse

Certain things remain
in the kingdom of the fathers—
        the driveway
    with its splats of gravel

and ruts filling with autumn rain,
        cold polio rain
    that capsizes the matchstick
mast and softening cereal-

        board keel. Their
    clipper's run afoul
of a spirea spine dropped from
        the bundle of debris

    they carted to the curb
earlier in the day, before the rain
        came to enlarge
    the kingdom. Aground. Marooned.

The Winston filter, dead captain,
        is wrapped in a leaf
    and lowered over the side
into the water; the dirge sounded

        on a grass
    blade, the salute given
and returned, and given again. Don't
        let the day

end, the volley thunders.
Let lightning approximate the light.
            But on the far
        shore, on the back-porch steps,

the radiant figure stands
            with its terrible offer:
        rescue, succor.
Demanding that other fealty.

Circadian

I.
The yellow stars of day lilies
        stand like Jews in the garden
next to the plantain
        lilies whose blossoms
are not forced to close
        against the dark, whose

orange badges are the identity
        cards
of the accepted order.
        I weed around them,
careful, respecting the hegemony
        laid out by the woman

who gardened here fifty
        years, who
knew about such things.
        There's something
of the Midwestern
        winter's lengthening

shadows, all that interior
        time, evident
in the beds. Stasis followed
        by daylit frenzy,
unchecked except by
        the ineluctable rhythms

of what blooms when. Perennials,
    all of them.
And nothing white. Not peonies,
    snowdrops, gardenias,
none of the black on white,
    white on gray tectonics

of the prison months, an
    evidence-by-absence
of what winter must have been
    for her. Lilies hard by
lilies. Deep into August,
    all those yellow stars . . .

    2.
In our bodies, too, stars
    wheel just beyond our
comprehension—in the blood
    to the cornea, in
the sudden dark. The scientists
    of sleep

say there is a somatic
    chemistry which paralyzes
the central nervous system
    so the mind, during dreams,
can't harm the body.
    And we wake up starred

by a journey our limbs
        weren't part of. Sun, which
we call consciousness or reason,
        draws us into the sphere
of reason, if we live in a
        lucky time. The screen door

bangs behind us, the embolic
        star forgotten
in the clutter of the potting shed,
        not yet ready
to enter the senses. It's the Zen
        of weeding, of deadheading

and pruning that convinces us
        solitude is possible,
that we are history-less.
        Which is why the garden
is dangerous, and the body,
        and has always been so.

        3.
There won't be a knock at the door
        for us, a midnight siege.
Our children will grow up
        in this house immunized
against polio and smallpox,
        and will leave here

and return, and leave again.
    The nuclear wind from Chernobyl
And Pennsylvania will have
    tested out, assimilated.
No one will walk in black shoes
    anymore. No one.

And at the end there will be
    someplace like this,
white pillars on a gray porch,
    ferns and sweet william
carpeting the shade. You can open
    the door into this hallway

and look at the unsilvering mirror's
    grainy spots,
dime-sized and flecked with rust,
    which send you back
an older self. And in the vase,
    the six points of the day

lily, sepal and petal three times
    repeated. "Hemerocallis,"
it's called, Greek for "beauty
    one evening." Not because it's most
beautiful at its vanishing, but because
    we were given one evening to see.

About the author

Lynne McMahon is a graduate of the University of California, Irvine (B.A. 1978) and the University of Utah (Ph.D. 1982). She was twice a winner of an Academy of American Poets Prize, at Irvine in 1978 and at Utah in 1981. Her chapbook, *White Tablecloths,* won the 1983 Riverstone International Chapbook Competition. McMahon is visiting professor of English at the University of Missouri-Columbia. She is married to Sherod Santos, who is also a Wesleyan poet.

About the book

This book was composed on the Mergenthaler 202 in Galliard, a contemporary rendering of a classic typeface prepared for Mergenthaler in 1978 by the British type designer Matthew Carter. The book was composed by G & S Typesetters of Austin, Texas, and designed and produced by Kachergis Book Design, Pittsboro, North Carolina.